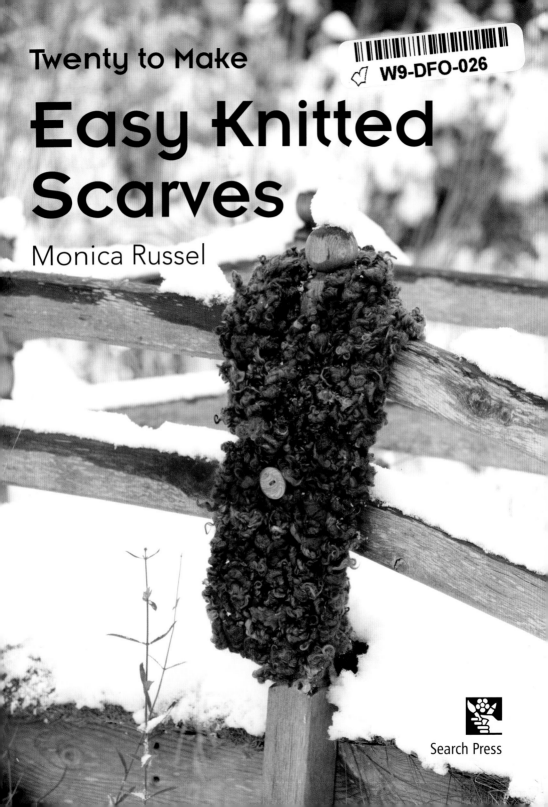

Twenty to Make

Easy Knitted Scarves

Monica Russel

Search Press

First published in Great Britain 2013

Search Press Limited
Wellwood, North Farm Road,
Tunbridge Wells, Kent TN2 3DR

Reprinted 2014

Text copyright © Monica Russel 2013

Photographs by Paul Bricknell at Search Press
studios and on location

Photographs and design copyright
© Search Press Ltd 2013

Print ISBN: 978-1-84448-911-4
EPUB ISBN: 978-1-78126-175-0
Mobi ISBN: 978-1-78126-176-7
PDF ISBN: 978-1-78126-177-4

The Publishers and author can accept no
responsibility for any consequences arising from
the information, advice or instructions given in
this publication.

Suppliers
If you have difficulty in obtaining any of the
materials and equipment mentioned in this book,
then please visit the Search Press website for
details of suppliers: www.searchpress.com

Printed in China

Dedication

*To Trevor, Matthew, Jacob,
Claerwen and Niloufer for their
continual encouragement and advice
for these projects; and to Chas and
Rachel and their herd of alpacas for
their generosity with yarns.*

Abbreviations

beg: beginning

DPN: double-pointed needles

g st: garter stitch: knit every row

inc: increase (by working into the front and
back of the stitch)

k: knit

k2tog: knit two stitches together

knitwise: as though to knit

m: make, usually make one additional stitch
by knitting into the front and back of the
same stitch

p: purl

p2tog: purl two stitches together

PM: place marker

psso: pass slipped stitch over

rem: remaining

rep: repeat

sl: slip, usually slip 1 stitch

st(s): stitch(es)

st st: stocking stitch (US stockinette stitch):
alternate knit and purl rows (unless directed
otherwise, always start with a knit row)

tbl: through back loop

WS: wrong side

wyrn: wrap yarn around needle to create an
extra stitch. (This makes up for the stitch you
lose when you knit two together.)

y/o: yarn over

*: repeat the instructions following the * as
many times as specified

Contents

Introduction

This book is a collection of knitting patterns for scarves. The patterns are easy to follow and are suitable for people who have mastered the basics in knitting. The scarves are practical and smart and the colours can be adapted to match your favourite garments. The diversity of the yarns makes the scarves suitable for all seasons.

The patterns in this book give the knitter the opportunity to try out new techniques such as cable knitting, making bobbles and simple lace. It also allows you to work in a range of yarns from a fine lace to a chunky alpaca. I have embellished some of the scarves with ribbons to add a different look.

My recent travels to Italy, Scotland and France inspired me to try new colours and textures and I had great fun knitting in cafés and working amongst rugged landscapes for some of the scarves.

This book has made me realise that scarves are not just for wrapping up in the depths of winter but, as accessories, can complement and enhance the appearance of many an outfit. I have especially enjoyed creating the lacier and lighter scarves.

There are scarves in this book for men, women and children, and for both the conventionally and unconventionally stylish. I hope you have hours of pleasure knitting them.

Whether you call them mufflers or scarves these wonderful examples of simple knitwear can be frivolous, functional and fun to wear. They will liven up a winter coat or add flair to a spring jacket as well as insulate you from the elements.
This picture shows just some of the scarves you can make with the instructions in this book – have fun!

Knitting know-how

General notes

The sizes of the scarves in the projects are for guidance and many of them can be adapted to suit your taste, making them suitable for all ages and heights. The patterns can be used for a number of projects and will develop your knowledge of knitting stitches.

Exact sizes are not needed to get a perfect end result, so you can repeat sections or add or remove rows to make them longer or shorter as you wish. The exceptions to this are the Red Rooster and Bow Tie scarves (see pages 20 and 30), the instructions for which must be followed more closely because of their shaping.

Yarn

All the scarves in this book have been knitted in natural fibres. I chose the yarns for their luxurious feel and quality but any comparable weight yarn can be substituted. It is advisable to check the length of yarn that you buy against the ones used in my patterns to ensure that you have enough to finish your scarf.

Yarns are available in balls, skeins and hanks. Balls and skeins of yarn are ready-wound so that you can immediately knit from them, while hanks are coils of yarn that need to be wound into a ball before use so that the yarn does not become tangled while you knit.

Yarn is bought in different weights and thicknesses. In some of the patterns lighter wool is used double to create a thicker yarn, and this is noted in the pattern.

• **Lace** weight, sometimes called 1, 2 or 3-ply, or cobweb, is a very fine yarn that is used for more open patterns. Generally one gets a sufficient length of yarn in a 50g ball or hank.

• **Double knitting** or **DK** yarn, is a medium thickness yarn that is suitable for many projects. The main DK yarn used in my projects is an alpaca with each ball containing 120m (131¼yd) of yarn.

• **Aran** yarn is thicker than DK and in this book there are 132m (144¼yd) of yarn per hank.

• **Chunky** and **super chunky** (US bulky) yarns are very thick. Each hank contains around 33m (36yd).

Tensions

These are very simple scarves and do not require you to make tension swatches. Each knitter will work slightly more tightly or loosely.

Needles

For these projects I used straight needles made from sustainable wood. I find these great to knit with because of their durability, and they are flexible to work with in all temperatures.

I used cable needles in some projects; these were also made from sustainable wood and are great to work with as the yarn does not fall off the needles.

All single-pointed needles come in pairs.

Other materials

For all of the projects you will need a pair of good quality sharp **scissors** to cut off the ends of yarns when sewing them into your work. You will also need scissors when making the pom poms for two of the projects in the book.

Stitch markers are needed for the pattern on page 30. They are used where a specific measurement is required within a pattern.

A **crochet hook** is used to help make tassels for some of the scarves.

This gorgeous scarf is a variation of the Pompom project on page 36, worked in emerald and parchment DK weight yarn.

Bobble

Materials:

5 x 50g balls of chunky (US bulky)
   yarn – Mist grey, 50–60m (55–66yd)

Needles:

1 pair of 7mm (UK 2; US 10½)
   single-pointed knitting needles

Large-eyed tapestry needle

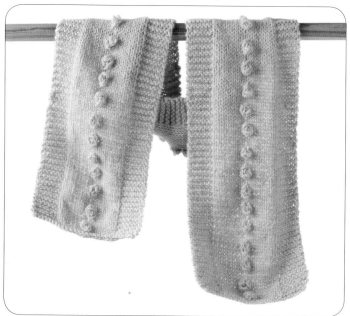

Instructions:

Bobble

To make bobble [MB]: (k1, y/o, k1, y/o, k1) into
next stitch, turn and p5, turn and k1, sl1, k2tog,
psso, k1, turn and p3tog.

When you have made the bobble, turn and knit
into the bobble st again in the main colour and
then continue knitting across the row.

Initial rows

Rows 1–2: Using 7mm (UK 2; US 10½) needles,
cast on 29sts in mist grey, then ktbl on return
row (i.e. row 2).

Main scarf pattern

Row 1: Knit.

Row 2 and all even rows: k7, p15, k7.

Row 3: k14, MB, k14.

Row 5: Knit.

Row 7: Knit.

Row 9: As row 3, MB.

Row 11: Knit.

Row 12: As row 2.

Continue with this twelve row pattern ten times
more and then repeat rows 1–11.

Next row: As row 2. Cast off.

Making up

Sew in loose ends on the wrong side of
your work.

This scarf has a really luxurious feel and will coordinate with all your winter clothes. The change of stitches adds style and the bobbles give the centre panel a focal point.

Ribs

Materials:
5 x 100g skeins of aran weight yarn –
variegated, 126m (137yd)

Needles:
1 pair of 5.5mm (UK 5; US 9) single-pointed
knitting needles

Large-eyed tapestry needle

5.5mm (UK 5, US 9/I) crochet hook

Instructions:

Initial rows
Rows 1–2: Using 5.5mm (UK 5; US 9)
needles, cast on 50sts in variegated yarn,
ktbl on return row (i.e. row 2).

Scarf pattern
Row 1: *k2, p2*, repeat from * to * to last
2 sts, k2.

Row 2: *p2, k2*, repeat from * to * to last
2sts, p2.

Repeat rows 1 and 2 until work measures
approximately 180cm (70¾in).

Cast off sts.

Making up
Sew in loose ends by weaving them into
your knitting.

Making tassels
Make 82 rounds of approximately 26cm
(10¼in) length to make the tassels.

Use your crochet hook to find the centre
of the raised part of each section of the rib,
then thread three doubled strands of wool
through to make each tassel. Neaten up
the tassels with scissors to ensure that they
are all the same length.

Knitting note
You can make tassels of the correct length by
wrapping the yarn around this book.

This is a really simple scarf to make once you have mastered the skills of purl and plain knitting. I have used a fairly chunky variegated yarn to make the texture more effective.

Heather & Skye

Materials:

1 x 250g skein super chunky (US super bulky) weight yarn – green/purple variegated, 220m (240½yd)

1 large wooden button

Purple darning yarn

Needles:

1 pair of 12mm (UK 000; US 17) single-pointed knitting needles

Large-eyed tapestry needle

Instructions:

Using 12mm (UK 000; US 17) needles, cast on 9sts in green/purple variegated yarn.

Scarf pattern

Row 1: k1, *wyrn, k2tog* repeat from * to *.

Next rows: Repeat row 1 until work measures 1m (39in).

Cast off sts.

In this pattern there are significant gaps between some stitches. Instead of making a specific buttonhole, one of these can be used when fastening the button.

Identify such a hole, then, in a position in which it can be fastened comfortably, sew on a button using purple darning yarn and the large-eyed tapestry needle.

Making up

Using your large-eyed needle sew in the ends of the yarn by weaving them into the rear of the scarf.

> **Knitting note**
>
> This was made using a handspun and dyed yarn from a cottage industry in Skye, Scotland. I simply knitted the scarf until the yarn ran out. The weight listed is therefore an estimate. Using an easily available bouclé super chunky yarn of approximately 250g and 200m (240½yd) will make a good substitute.

This scarf was inspired by a visit to Skye. I really loved the colours of the heathers and ferns and so bought handspun and locally dyed wool in colours to match them.

Frivolous Florence

Materials:

2 x 50g skeins lace weight – purple/
green variegated, 400m (437yd)

150cm (59in) ribbon for edging

Needles:

1 pair of 4mm (UK 8; US 6) single-
pointed knitting needles

Large-eyed tapestry needle

Instructions:

Using 4mm (UK 8; US 6) needles, cast on
52 sts in purple/green variegated yarn.

Scarf pattern

Row 1: Knit.

Row 2: Purl.

Row 3: k4, *y/o, sl1, k1, psso, k2tog, y/o, k4*, repeat from * to *.

Row 4: Purl.

Next rows: Rep rows 1–4 pattern until work measures 190cm
(74¾in).

Cast off sts.

Making up

Sew in loose ends by weaving them in at the side of the scarf.

Weave your ribbon into the holes like a running stitch.
Turn back the edge and using your knitting yarn and tapestry
needle make a neat hem at either side of the ribbon. Press the
scarf neatly.

This scarf was inspired by a visit to Tuscany. I have knitted it in a variegated lace yarn and then threaded some ribbons in at the ends to add a bit of chic. As with the other patterns the length and width can be altered to suit your taste. This scarf can be wrapped around the neck once or twice depending on the look wanted.

Steely Tweed

Materials:

9 x 50g balls of DK weight yarn – 4 x mid grey
  (A), 4 x parchment (B), 1 x black (C); all 132m
  (144yd)

CD case

Needles:

1 pair of 5mm (UK 6; US 8) single-pointed
knitting needles

Large-eyed tapestry needle

5mm (UK 6, US 8/H) crochet hook

Instructions:

Throughout the pattern, knit one strand of A
and one strand of B together to produce the
tweed effect.

Initial rows

Rows 1–2: Using 5mm (UK 6; US 8) needles cast
on 45 sts, ktbl on return row (i.e. row 2).

Scarf pattern

Rows 1 and 3: p3, *k1, sl1, k1, p3*, repeat from
* to * to end of row.

Rows 2 and 4: *k3, p1, k1, p1*, repeat from * to
* to last 3 sts, k3.

Rows 5 and 7: k4, *sl1, k5*, repeat from * to * to
last 4 sts, k4.

Rows 6 and 8: p4, *k1, p5*, repeat from * to * to
last 4 sts, p4.

Next rows: Continue knitting rows 1–8 until
scarf measures Cast off sts. Sew in loose sts by
weaving them into the knitting at the rear of work.

Making tassels

Wind black wool around the short sides of the CD case and cut it in the
centre to make lengths for the tassels.

   Use four strands at a time and a 5mm (UK 6, US 8/H) crochet hook to
thread the wool through the scarf to make seventeen tassels for each end.

A classic look that is knitted by using shades of alpaca wool together. Black tassels add interest.

Sumptuous

Materials:

1 x 100g hanks of 4-ply (fingering) yarn – fawn, 480m (525yd)

Needles:

1 pair of 4.5mm (UK 7; US 7) single-pointed knitting needles

1 pair of 5mm (UK 6; US 8) single-pointed knitting needles

Large-eyed tapestry needle

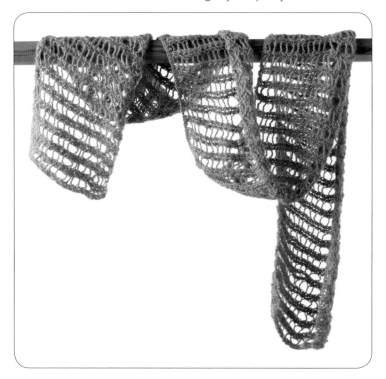

Instructions:

Using 5mm (UK 6; US 8) needles and fawn yarn, cast on 254 sts loosely. Change to 4.5mm (UK 7; US 7) needles.

Scarf pattern

Row 1: k1, *k2tog, y/o twice, k2tog*, repeat from * to * to last sts, k1.

Row 2: p1, *p2, k1, p1*, repeat from * to * to last st, p1.

Next rows: Repeat rows 1 and 2 until work measures 16.5cm (6½in).

Cast off sts using the 5mm (UK 6; US 8) needles.

Making up

Sew loose ends into the rear of your scarf with the tapestry needle.

This is a really useful accessory as it will keep the chill off autumn and spring days. I have knitted it in neutral colours that will fit in with most items of clothing. The pattern can be adapted for thicker yarns but I loved the feel of this fine alpaca. This is really easy to knit on straight needles. This scarf can be made longer and wider by adding more stitches and knitting additional rows.

Red Rooster

Materials:
2 x 100g hanks of aran weight yarn – red,
132m (144yd)

Needles:
1 pair of 5.5mm (UK 5; US 9) single-pointed
knitting needles

Large-eyed tapestry needle

1 cable needle

Knitting note
c6b: slip next 3 sts on to a cable needle and
hold at back of work, knit next 3 sts from left-
hand needle, then knit sts from cable needle.

c6f: (slip next 3 sts on to a cable needle and
hold at front of work, then knit next sts from
left-hand needle)

Instructions:

Initial rows
Rows 1–2: Using 5.5mm (UK 5; US 9) needles,
cast on 46sts in red, ktbl on return row
(i.e. row 2).

Double cable pattern
Row 1: p5, k36, p5.

Row 2: k5, p36, k5.

Row 3: p5, c6b, c6f. Repeat the twelve-stitch
cable pattern twice more, p5.

Row 4: k5, p36, k5.

Rows 5 and 6: As rows 1 and 2.

Repeat the above six rows until work measures
82cm (32¼in), then repeat rows 1–4 once more.
Cast off sts.

Making up
Measure 12cm (4¾in) from the cast-on/cast off
edges. Using a piece of yarn, gather the end
of the scarf in, and wrap the wool several times
around the middle tightly. Tie a knot and sew
in any loose ends. Fan your knitting out to form
your edge.

Making the bow
Using 5.5mm (UK 5; US 9) needles, cast on 16
sts in red.

Rows 1–16: Knit (garter stitch).

Cast off sts.

Fold knitting in half lengthways (short ends
together). Using your tapestry needle and a
piece of yarn do a series of running sts along
the centre line and draw them in tightly to form
the centre of the bow. Sew in your loose ends
of yarn.

Completing the scarf
Cut six lengths of yarn, each measuring
approximately 76cm (30in). Tie a knot at one
end to hold the pieces together. Make a long
plait using the strands in three pairs. Fold the
completed plait in half and tie it around the
centre of the bow.

To wear the scarf, wrap it around your neck
crossing the two ends over each other. Hold the
bow over the centre and tie the plaits together.

This is a very neat little scarf that will add fun and style to your wardrobe. For a different look change the central bow and add a large brooch. The scarf is easy to make once you have learnt how to cable.

Fuchsia

Materials:

2 x 100g skeins of aran weight yarn – fuchsia
  pink, 126m (138yd)

Needles:

1 pair of 8mm (UK 0; US 11) circular needles

Large-eyed tapestry needle

Instructions:

Initial rows

Rows 1–2: Using 8mm (UK 0; US 11) needles,
cast on 178 sts in fuchsia pink, ktbl on return
row (i.e. row 2).

Scarf pattern

Row 1: *k2, p2*, rep from * to * to the end of
the row.

Rows 2–4: Rep row 1 three more times (this
pattern is called moss stitch).

Row 5: *k1, wyrn*, rep from * to * to the last st.

Row 6: *k1, drop the wrapped st off the
needle*, rep from * to *, knit the last st.

Rows 7–8: Rep rows 5 and 6.

Rows 9–10: Knit.

Rows 11–28: Rep rows 5–10 three more times.

Rows 29–32: *k2, p2*, rep from * to * to the end
of the row. Cast off sts.

Making up

Using your tapestry needle, weave in the loose
ends of the yarn.

This is a scarf with a twist as it is knitted using circular needles as a long needle. The scarf can be knitted to any length simply by adjusting the number of cast-on stitches and the number of rows knitted.

Twister

Materials:
1 x 100g hank of DK yarn –
    variegated, 270m (295yd)

Needles:
1 pair of 4mm (UK 8; US 6) single-
    pointed knitting needles

Large-eyed tapestry needle

Instructions:

Initial rows
Rows 1–2: Using 4mm (UK 8; US 6) needles, cast on 20 sts in variegated yarn, ktbl on return row (i.e. row 2).

Scarf pattern
Row 1: k8, turn, k8.

Row 2: k6, turn, k6.

Row 3: k4, turn, k4.

Row 4: Knit across 20 sts on needle.

Repeat rows 1–4 until approximately 1m (39in) of the yarn is left.

Cast off the 20 sts, then use the large-eyed embroidery needle to sew in the ends of the yarn.

This is a really simple scarf that has a twist created by knitting different numbers of stitches into the rows. I have chosen a lovely variagated merino and silk yarn in a summery colours but it could equally be knitted in another soft yarn.

Autumnal

Materials:

6 x 50g balls of DK yarn – 2 x orange (A), 2 x red
(B), 2 x cream (C); all 132m (144yd)

Needles:

1 pair of 4mm (UK 8; US 6) single-pointed
knitting needles

Large-eyed tapestry needle

Instructions:

Initial rows

Rows 1–2: Using 4mm (UK 8; US 6) needles,
cast on 50 sts in yarn A, ktbl on return row (i.e.
row 2).

Scarf pattern

Row 1: Knit.

Row 2: Purl.

Repeat rows 1 and 2 once more. Join in yarn B.

Rows 5–10: Work st st in B. Join in yarn C.

Rows 11–14: Work st st in C. Change to yarn B.

Rows 15–18: Work st st in B. Change to yarn A.

Rows 19–22: Work st st in A. Change to yarn C.

Rows 23–28: Work st st in yarn C.

Rows 29–84: Repeat rows 1–28 twice more. Cut
off yarns B and C.

Rows 85–98: Work st st in yarn A, cut off yarn.

Rows 99–112: Rejoin yarn B and work st st, cut
off yarn.

Rows 113–126: Rejoin yarn C and work st st, cut
off yarn.

Next rows: Repeat the above sequence of
fourteen row sections seven more times and
then one more stripe in colour A.

Next rows: Continue with the smaller stripes
ensuring they match the order of the ones
worked at the start of the pattern (this will
mean reversing the order). Start with four rows
of colour C.

At the end of the three repeats of the twenty-
eight row sequence, cast off your stitches.

Making up

Use the large-eyed embroidery needle to sew
in the ends of the yarn.

This scarf is going to be a welcome addition to any autumn/winter wardrobe. I have used stripes to add interest. Choose bright colours or subtle colours to match your winter coat or jacket.

Rasta

Materials:

12 x 50g balls of DK yarn – 3 x green (A), 3 x yellow (B), 3 x black (C), 3 x red (D); all 100m (109yd)

Needles:

1 pair of 5.5mm (UK 5; US 9) single-pointed knitting needles

Large-eyed tapestry needle

Instructions:

Use the yarns doubled throughout the pattern.

Bobble

To make bobble [MB]: (k1, y/o, k1, y/o, k1) into next stitch, turn and p5, turn and k1, sl1, k2tog, psso, k1, turn and p3tog.

Shaped border

Row 1: Using 5.5mm (UK 5; US 9) needles and yarn A cast on 1 st and MB into the same st.

Row 2: inc 1, k1.

Row 3: inc 1, k2.

Row 4: inc 1, k3.

Next rows: Carry on increasing in this way until there are 11 sts on your needle.

Next 2 rows: Knit in the same yarn. Cut off yarn.

Repeat the above rows with each of the other three yarns (B, C and D). There will now be 44 sts on your needle.

Scarf pattern section 1

Rows 1–10: Using yarn D knit across all sts, twisting in ends of each colour so that there are no gaps in the work.

Rows 11–20: Join in yarn C and knit (twist in yarn D at the end of alternate rows so there are no large loops at the end of the rows).

Rows 21–30: Join in yarn B and knit (twist in yarns D and C so there are no large loops at the end of rows.

Rows 31–40: Join in yarn A and knit (twist in yarns B, C and D so there are no large loops at the ends of rows).

Repeat rows 1–40 once more.

Scarf pattern section 2

Rows 1–8: Using yarn D knit across all sts, twisting in ends of each colour so that there are no gaps in the work.

Rows 9–16: Join in yarn C and knit (twist in yarn D at the end of alternate rows so there are no large loops at the end of the rows).

Rows 17–24: Join in yarn B and knit (twist in yarns D and C so there are no large loops at the end of rows).

Rows 25–32: Join in yarn A and knit (twist in yarns B, C and D so there are no large loops at the ends of rows).

Repeat rows 1–32 twice more.

Scarf pattern section 3

Rows 1–80: Repeat rows 1–40 of scarf pattern section 1 twice more.

Rows 81–144: Repeat rows 1–32 of scarf pattern section 2 twice more.

Repeat rows 1–144 until the work measures 180cm (70¾in), ending with an eight row stripe in yarn D.

End border

Next rows: k11, turn, k11, turn, k2tog, knit to end, turn, k2tog, knit to end. Repeat until you have 1 st on your needle.

With right side facing, MB. Cut off yarn, rejoin yarn C and follow the above sequence. Rejoin yarn B and complete the above sequence. Rejoin yarn A and complete the above sequence.

Making up

Sew in all loose ends by weaving them into the back of the scarf.

This is a fun scarf that I have knitted in bright colours but could equally be knitted in a plain colour for a different feel. It would be a great scarf to wear at a festival.

Bow Tie

Materials:
2 x 50g balls of DK yarn – ochre, 132m (144yd)

Two stitch markers

Needles:
1 pair of 4.5mm (UK 7; US 7) single-pointed knitting needles

Large-eyed tapestry needle

Instructions:
Using 4.5mm (UK 7; US 7) needles and ochre yarn, cast on 21 sts.

Scarf section 1
Row 1: inc 1, knit to last 4 sts, sl1, k1, psso, k2.

Row 2: k3, purl to last 3 sts, k3.

Next rows: Repeat rows 1 and 2 until work measures 16.5cm (6½in) ending with a wrong side row.

Scarf section 2
Row 1: k2, k2tog, knit to last 4 sts, sl1, k1, psso, k2.

Row 2: k3, purl to last 3 sts, k3.

Next rows: Repeat rows 1 and 2 until there are 9sts remaining on your needle ending with a wrong side row.

Scarf section 3
Row 1: inc 1, knit to last 2 sts, inc 1, k1.

Row 2: k3, purl to last 3 sts, k3.

Next rows: Repeat rows 1 and 2 until you have 37 sts on your needle, ending with a wrong side row.

Scarf section 4
Row 1: Knit.

Row 2: k3, purl to last 3 sts, k3.

Row 3: Inc 1, knit to last 2 sts, inc 1, k1.

Row 4: As row 2.

Scarf section 5
Place a marker at each side of scarf.

Row 1: Knit.

Row 2: k3, purl to last 3 sts, k3.

Next rows: Repeat rows 1 and 2 for 10cm (4in) from your marker ending with a wrong side row.

Scarf section 6
Row 1: k2, k2tog, knit to the last 4 sts, sl1, k1, psso, k2.

Row 2: k3, purl to last 3 sts, k3.

Row 3: Knit.

Row 4: k3, purl to the last 3 sts, k3.

Next rows: Repeat rows 1–4 until you have 37sts remaining on your needle, ending with a row 4 of the pattern.

Scarf section 7
As section 2 but only until there are 19sts remaining on your needle, ending with a wrong side row. Place marker to denote start of neck.

Scarf section 8
As section 5 until work measures 40cm (15¾in) from your marker. Repeat sections 3–6 once.

Scarf section 9
Row 1: k2, k2tog, k to last 4 sts, sl1, k1, psso, k2.

Row 2: k3, purl to last 3 sts, k3.

Repeat rows 1 and 2 until there are 9sts remaining on your needle, ending with a wrong side row.

Scarf section 10
Work as for scarf section 3 until you have 23 sts on your needle.

Scarf section 11

Place marker.

Row 1: k2, k2tog, knit to last 2 sts, inc 1, k1.

Row 2: k3, purl to last 3 sts, k3.

Next rows: Repeat rows 1 and 2 until work measures 16.5cm (6½in) from your marker. Cast off remaining sts.

Making up

Sew in any loose ends at the rear of your scarf using the tapestry needle, then lightly press your knitting.

This is a very feminine scarf that has a vintage feel to it. Wrap the middle section around your neck and make a bow with the right side facing. I like to have the bow at the side of my neck but you can play around to place it where you would like it. You could also use the scarf as a belt for a knitted dress.

Parisienne Chic

Materials:

2 x 50g hanks of lace weight
  yarn – light pink, 400m
  (437yd)

Needles:

1 pair of 4mm (UK 8; US 6) single-
  pointed knitting needles

Large-eyed tapestry needle

Instructions:

Initial rows

Rows 1–2: Using 4mm (UK 8;
US 6) needles and pink yarn,
cast on 56 sts, ktbl on return
row (i.e. row 2).

Scarf pattern

Rows 1–4: Knit.

Row 5: *k1, wyrn*, repeat from
* to * until the last stitch, k1.

Row 6: k1, drop the stitch you
wrapped in the previous row.

Next rows: Repeat rows 1–6
until you have knitted 184cm
(72½in), finishing with four
rows of garter stitch.

Cast off sts.

Making up

Sew in all your loose ends by
using the tapestry needle to
weave them into your knitting.

This is a simple scarf that has been knitted in a very fine lace yarn. You can drape it in many ways and it will be a great asset to a spring or summer wardrobe.

Candy Stripe

Materials:

5 x 50g balls of DK yarn – 2 x midnight blue
(A), 2 x rose (B), 1 x parchment (C); all 132m
(144yd)

Needles:

1 pair of 3.75mm (UK 9; US 5) single-pointed
knitting needles

Large-eyed tapestry needle

Instructions:

Initial rows

Rows 1–2: Using 3.75mm (UK 9; US 5) needles
and yarn A, cast on 41 sts, ktbl on return row
(i.e. row 2).

Scarf pattern

Rows 1–2: Work g st (this is knitting every row).

Rows 3–4: Work st st.

Rows 5–8: Change to yarn B, work st st.

Rows 9–10: Change to yarn C, work st st.

Rows 11–16: Change to yarn A, work st st.

Repeat rows 5–16 until work measures 112cm
(44in), ending with a stripe in yarn C.

Next 2 rows: Change to yarn A, work st st.

Next 4 rows: Change to yarn A, work g st.

Cast off sts.

Making up

Sew in all your loose ends by using the tapestry
needle to weave them into your knitting.

Knitting note

Twist the yarn every second row to avoid
large loops as you knit the scarf.

I have knitted this scarf for a child but the pattern can be adjusted to fit an adult. Colours can be chosen to suit your preferences.

Pompom

Materials:

5 x 50g balls of DK yarn – 4 x sapphire (A), 1 x parchment (B); all 132m (144yd)

2 pieces of card and scissors to make circles for the pompoms

Needles:

1 pair of 5mm (UK 6; US 8) single-pointed knitting needles

Large-eyed tapestry needle

Instructions:

Initial rows

Rows 1–2: Using 5mm (UK 6; US 8) needles and yarn A cast on 42 sts, ktbl on return row (i.e. row 2).

Scarf pattern

Row 1: (right side) *p3, k3*, repeat from * to * until the end of the row.

Row 2: Knit.

Next rows: Repeat rows 1 and 2 until work measures 170cm (67in).

Cast off sts.

Pompom (make four)

1 Cut out two identical 3.25cm (1¼in) diameter circles of cardboard.

2 Cut a 1.5cm (½in) diameter round hole in the middle of each circle.

3 Holding the two rings of cardboard together, wind yarn B evenly and tightly round and round, passing each winding through the hole in the middle and over the outer edge of the cardboard ring until the hole is filled with yarn.

4 Carefully cut through the yarn at the outer edge of the rings, making sure that all the yarn remains in place.

5 Take a piece of matching yarn and wind it between the two outer rings. Tie this tightly around the centre of the two rings with two knots to secure.

6 Remove your pompom from the cardboard rings and roll it around in your hands to make it fluffy. Trim the edges to even them out.

Making up

Use the tapestry needle to sew in all ends of wool by weaving them into the sts on the rear of your scarf.

Sew a pompom into each corner of your scarf using spare yarn and the tapestry needle.

Knitting note

Threading a darning needle with the yarn to wind the wool around the rings makes it much easier.

This is a really simple scarf adding
a twist to a basic rib. I have added
contrasting pompoms to add a bit of
fun. As with the other scarves, the size
can be altered to suit your needs.

Simple Lace

Materials:

2 x 100g hanks of DK silk blend wool – variegated green/blue, 270m (295yd)

Needles:

1 pair of 4.5mm (UK 7; US 7) single-pointed knitting needles

Large-eyed tapestry needle

Instructions:

Initial rows

Rows 1–2: Using 4.5mm (UK 7; US 7) needles cast on 47 sts in variegated green/blue, ktbl on return row (i.e. row 2).

Scarf pattern

Row 1: Knit (right side).

Row 2: Purl.

Row 3: (right side) k2, *yfwd, k2tog, k1*, repeat from * to * until end of row.

Row 4: Purl.

Repeat rows 1–4 until work measures 182cm (71½in).

Cast off sts.

Making up

Sew in loose ends using the tapestry needle.

This scarf will suit all seasons as it is made from a mixture of merino wool and silk. It is made from a very simple lace stitch and the length and width can be adapted to suit your taste.

Autumn Haze

Materials:

3 x 100g hanks of DK silk
    blend yarn – variegated
    fawn/grey, 270m (295yd)

Needles:

1 pair of 7mm (UK 2; US 10½) single-
    pointed knitting needles

Large-eyed tapestry needle

Instructions:

Use the yarns tripled throughout the pattern.

Initial rows

Rows 1–2: Using 7mm (UK 2; US 10½) needles and variegated
fawn/grey yarn, cast on 16 sts, then ktbl on return row (i.e. row 2).

Scarf pattern

Rows 1 and 2: *k2, p2*, repeat to end.

Rows 3 and 4: *p2, k2*, repeat to end.

Repeat rows 1–4 until work measures approximately 156cm
(61½in).

Cast off sts.

Making up

Sew in loose ends using the tapestry needle.

This is a really simple scarf that is made in variegated wool used quadruple, which adds texture to the stitch. The scarf uses a simple moss stitch knitted on large needles.

College Stripe

Materials:

4 x 50g balls of DK yarn – 3 x grey (A), 1 x rust (B); all 132m (144yd)

Needles:

1 pair of 5mm (UK 6; US 8) single-pointed knitting needles

Large-eyed tapestry needle

Instructions:

Use the yarns doubled throughout the pattern.

Using 5mm (UK 6; US 8) needles and yarn A cast on 220 sts.

Rows 1–3: *k2, p2*, repeat from * to * until end of the row. Change to yarn B.

Row 4: Knit.

Row 5: Purl.

Rows 6–7: Repeat rows 4 and 5, cut off yarn B.

Rows 8–29: Using yarn A, work st st. Change to yarn B.

Rows 30–33: Work st st, cut off yarn B.

Row 34: Knit one row using yarn A.

Rows 35–37: Repeat rows 1–3. Cast off sts.

Making up

Sew in loose ends by weaving them into the back of your scarf.

This is a really easy scarf that I have knitted using 35.5cm (14in) straight needles but it could equally be knitted using circular needles by using them in the same way as you would straight ones. The pattern was inspired by the classical college stripe although I have only used two colours. You could do this using many colours to form vertical stripes once the stitches are cast off.

Zebra Razzle

Materials:

4 x 50g balls of DK yarn – 2 x black (A),
   2 x parchment (B); all 132m (144yd)

Needles:

1 pair of 4.5mm (UK 7; US 7) single-pointed
   knitting needles

1 pair of 4mm (UK 8; US 6) single-pointed
   knitting needles

Large-eyed tapestry needle

Instructions:

Initial rows

Rows 1–2: Using 4mm (UK 8; US 6) needles and
yarn A cast on 49 sts, ktbl on return row (i.e.
row 2).

Rib section

Row 1: *k1, p1*, repeat to last st, k1.

Row 2: *p1, k1*, repeat to last st, p1.

Rows 3–4: Repeat rows 1 and 2.

Stripe pattern section

Change to 4.5mm (UK 7; US 7) needles.

Row 1: To set the pattern, purl 1 row in colour A.

Row 2: (Right side) Using colour B, (k1, sl1) 5
times; *k10, sl1, (k1, sl1) 4 times*, repeat * to *
once more to last st, k1.

Row 3: Using colour B, (p1, sl1) 5 times, *p10,
sl1 (p1, sl1) 4 times*, repeat from * to * once
more to last st, p1.

Row 4: Using colour A, k2, sl1, (k1, sl1) 3 times;
k12, sl1, (k1, sl1) 3 times, repeat * to * once
more to last 2 sts, k2.

Row 5: Using colour A, p2, sl1, (p1, sl1) 3 times;
p12, sl1, (p1, sl1) 3 times, repeat * to * once
more to last 2 sts, p2.

Next rows: Continue in set pattern (rows 2–5
only) until work measures approximately 158cm
(62¼in), ending with a row 5. Cut off yarn B.

Next row: Change to size 4mm (UK 8; US 6)
needles and knit in yarn A.

Next 4 rows: Work rows 1–4 of the rib section
as you did at the start of the scarf.

Cast off your stitches.

Making up

Sew in loose ends by weaving them into the
back of your scarf.

44

This is a funky little scarf that cleverly ruches in panels. I have made it in traditional black and white using ultra-soft alpaca wool.

Bolero

Materials:

4 x 100g hanks of super chunky (super bulky) yarn – turquoise, 32m (35yd)

2 pieces of card and scissors to make circles for the pompoms

Needles:

1 pair of 9mm (UK 00; US 13) single-pointed knitting needles

Large-eyed tapestry needle

Instructions:

Scarf section 1

Using 9mm (UK 00; US 13) needles and turquoise yarn, cast on 3 sts.

Row 1: Knit.

Row 2: k1, m1, k1, m1, k1.

Row 3: Knit.

Row 4: k1, m1, k3, m1, k1.

Row 5: Knit.

Row 6: k1, m1, k5, m1, k1.

Row 7: Knit.

Row 8: k1, m1, k7, m1, k1.

Row 9: Knit.

Row 10: k1, m1, k9, m1, k1.

Row 11: Knit.

Row 12: k1, m1, k11, m1, k1.

Row 13: Knit.

Row 14: Purl.

Rows 15–20: Repeat rows 13 and 14 three more times.

Rows 21–22: Knit.

Scarf section 2

Rows 1–8: Work st st.

Rows 9–10: Knit.

Repeat rows 1–10 until work measures 125cm (49¼in) , ending with knit 2 rows.

Decreasing rows

Odd numbered rows: k2tog, knit to last 2 sts, k2tog.

Even numbered rows: Knit.

Continue knitting until there are 3 sts left ending with an even numbered row.

Cast off sts.

Making up

Make two bobbles from turquoise yarn, following the instructions on page 36, using 5.25cm (2in) cardboard circles with 2.5cm (1in) holes in the centre. Sew in all your loose ends by using the tapestry needle to weave them into your knitting. Using the yarn from your pompoms, attach one to the cast-on edge and one to the decreased edge of your scarf.

This is an extremely simple scarf that will keep you very cosy on a winter's day. It can be knitted over an evening or two.

Acknowledgements

Thanks to Rachel at UK Alpaca, Jenny at
Artesano and Ruth at The Little Wool Company
for supplying me with some of the yarns.
Also my appreciation to Search Press for asking
me to do the designs for this book and to all my
knitting students who have inspired me.
You are invited to visit the author's website:
www.theknitknacks.co.uk

Publishers' Note

If you would like more information on knitting techniques, try:
Knitting for the Absolute Beginner by Alison Dupernex,
Search Press, 2012;
Twenty to Make: Knitted Boot Cuffs by Monica Russel,
Search Press, 2012